RAINBOW ROOSTER
COLORS O'AHU
A LOCAL'S GUIDE

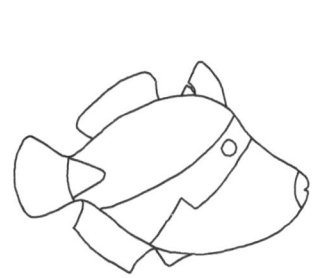

SAM AND ROBERT CHEN
ART BY WAIBUN AND EMILY LEE

RAINBOW ROOSTER COLORS O'AHU: A LOCAL'S GUIDE

To my mom, for creating me.
To my 阿公 and 阿嬤 for introducing me to all the wonders of O'ahu.
To my 公公 and 婆婆 for always supporting me.
            –S.C.

To my mom, my two sisters and my dad.
            –W.B.L.

For XSS: dreams are possible.
            –R.C.

For Mom and Dad. The best is yet to come.
            –E.L.

First Edition: December 2025
Printing: IngramSpark (Tennessee, USA)

Connect with us!
Web: HIRAINBOWROOSTER.COM
Email: INFO@HIRAINBOWROOSTER.COM
Instagram: @HIRAINBOWROOSTER

ISBN: 979-8-9934654-8-7

THIS BOOK BELONGS TO

_____

MY COLOR PALETTE

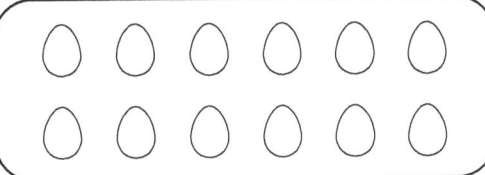

TABLE OF CONTENTS

INTRODUCTION – LET'S HATCH SOME FUN TOGETHER!

Aloha from Rainbow Rooster!

Cock-a-doodle-doo! Aloha and welcome to one of the most magical islands in the world: O'ahu! My name is Rainbow Rooster, and I'll be your expert chicken guide. As a local resident of this beautiful paradise, I'm so excited to share with you all my favorite things to do on O'ahu.

What you'll find inside

When I travel, I love experiencing new places as a local. Using this guide book, I hope you'll learn to enjoy O'ahu **the local way**. Follow me as I reveal **hidden gems** that are off the beaten tourist path. With me as your guide, you'll be able to explore a mansion next to Diamond Head that's full of Islamic art, kayak to a sandbar that disappears and reappears with the tides, and see a replica of a thousand-year old Japanese temple.

As you visit famous sites on your itinerary, I'll be here to guide you. For example, at Hanauma Bay, I'll share **fun facts** like the story of the bay's infamous "Toilet Bowl," **tips** to avoid having mongooses ruin your day, and fun **anecdotes** like the friendly monk seal I once met there.

As a chicken, I live for food! You can count on my **food recommendations** for restaurants and snacks that locals love. From my favorite shave ice order (Strawberry Dream) to my favorite crack seed snack (Li Hing Sour Lychee), you'll be ready to enjoy the food paradise that is O'ahu.

Toward the end of the book, you will discover **island insights** pages that will answer interesting questions like how American sweets led to the end of the Hawaiian Kingdom.

Color this book with your own experiences!

By the end of your trip, I hope you'll have seen enough of O'ahu to recognize most of the things in this book. Best of all, as you read about these places, there are hand-drawn illustrations (made by my uncle and cousin) waiting for you to fill with color from your own experiences to make it an even more memorable visit.

HOW TO USE THIS BOOK

Monk seal (17)

In the egg, write
the page where
you found the symbol!

hirainbowrooster.com

Egg hunt: Find the symbols of Hawai'i!

I've created a game for you! Toward the back of the book, you'll see two pages of Hawaiian symbols and icons—common things you might see on your trip to O'ahu. To make things fun, I've hidden them in the illustrations for you to find. Look for the nine **Official Hawai'i State Symbols** and the nine **Unofficial Hawai'i Icons** as you color your way through the book. When you find the hidden symbol, write down the egg number you found it on!

Visit our website for our Hawaiian music playlist, and more!

In the *Book Extras* section of our website, *hirainbowrooster.com* (or use the QR code to the left), you'll find content to enrich your travel experience. For example, you'll find the **answers to the egg hunt**, the Spotify **Rainbow Rooster playlist** of Hawaiian music that my cousin Emily created for you to enjoy as you color these illustrations, and other travel resources. Access our **map guides** that show you the exact locations of the 28 attractions and my 100+ recommendations right on your phone.

Learn some Hawaiian words

At the bottom of each O'ahu attraction page, there's a Hawaiian word or phrase for you to learn. There are only 12 letters in the Hawaiian alphabet and the sounds are simple, so give it a try! (Pay attention to the apostrophes, which signal a pause in the word and can change its meaning—which is why Oahu is properly spelled O'ahu.) Signs with Hawaiian words are all over the island, so learning them could help you navigate around the island and understand the local culture.

LEARN HAWAIIAN
e komo mai *(e KOH-mo MY)* – welcome

MY TUTU'S HOUSE
@ EAST HONOLULU (Aina Haina)

Welcome to O'ahu! When I visit Hawai'i, I often stay with my tutu (grandparents) in Honolulu. I love to spend my vacations here because there are so many different things to do. My favorites include swimming in the ocean, catching fish, building sand castles, and eating shave ice, all of which I learned to do right here. Most of all, I love spending time with my family, and I hope you will meet some locals who will feel like part of your **ohana** too. If you've seen the TV show *Hawai'i Five-O*, you might be interested to know that my grandparents live a couple doors down from McGarrett's house.

LEARN HAWAIIAN
'ohana (*oh-HAH-nah*) – family

DON'T MISS NEARBY

Kahala Beach
The beach in front of the Kahala has the finest-grained sand on O'ahu and protection from waves, making it a favorite among younger swimmers. Check out Magic Island for another kid-friendly beach.

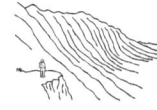

Kuli'ou'ou Ridge Trail
The altitude and shade will keep you cool while you hike for a reward: the beautiful view of the windward side of the island.

Kahala Mall
Shop with the locals! Stop by my favorite art gallery, Nohea Gallery, and great local stores like Up & Riding, SoHa, and Reyn Spooner.

Hawai'i Costcos
Costcos here stock useful local items like water gear (snorkels, kayaks) and gifts for the folks back home (Hawaiian cookies, chocolates, and nuts).

Kaimuki restaurants
This area is Hawai'i's foodie capital! My favorites include Pig & the Lady, Totoya, and Mud Hen Water.

BYODO-IN TEMPLE
@ WINDWARD (Kaneohe)

This Buddhist temple is a little slice of Japan on Oʻahu. In fact, it's a copy of the original Byodo-In Temple located near Kyoto. Although this one was built more than 50 years ago, the original was built over one thousand years ago, without nails, hammers, concrete, or other modern tools. This **heiau** is beautifully set against the Koʻolau mountains, and many TV shows and movies filmed on Oʻahu use it as a setting. My favorite thing to do here is to see the beautiful koi fish, who are eager to greet you, whether or not you bought fish food from the gift shop.

DON'T MISS NEARBY

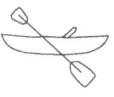

Kaneohe sandbar
This sandbar in the bay disappears and reappears with the tides. A fun day trip by kayak or boat (I prefer kayak!) for snorkeling and island fun with amazing views.

Hoomaluhia Botanical Gardens
Beautiful gardens make for picture-perfect photos, featuring beautiful lakes full of more eager orange fish—not koi, but cichlid—against the Koʻolau mountains.

Olomana Trail (Three Peaks)
A very difficult hike that rewards you with spectacular views of the Koʻolau on one side and the perfect Kailua and Waimanalo beaches on the other.

Food recommendation
Fresh Catch is a great hole-in-the-wall for all kinds of local-style poke.

LEARN HAWAIIAN
heiau (HEH-ow) – shrine

CHINATOWN
@ DOWNTOWN HONOLULU

Honolulu's Chinatown is the oldest one in the United States, and it is still very busy today. You'll find many open markets selling all sorts of fruits, vegetables, and (still-squirming!) fish. Be sure to stop for sugar cane juice or a smoothie to cool yourself down. Chinatown is known for a plentiful selection of restaurants, food factories, art galleries and flower shops. **Pake** and other locals buy leis here for many occasions, from graduations to retirement parties to welcoming visitors. They look great and can smell great too!

DON'T MISS BEST EATS IN CHINATOWN

Sing Cheong Yuan
A Chinese bakery selling local manapua (the Hawaiian version of char siu bao, meat wrapped in buns) and other dim sum treats.

Pho To Chau
A hole-in-the-wall with the most authentic Vietnamese noodles this side of the Pacific!

Maguro Brothers
Fresh seafood over rice, my favorite! The fish is among the freshest you can buy.

Chi Kong Look Funn Factory
Chinatown used to be full of factories like this one churning out authentic dim sum. The char siu rolls are especially tasty.

Chau's Fresh Fruit
You might need a juice or smoothie to cool down, and this is the place to get it!

LEARN HAWAIIAN
pake *(PAH-keh)* – a chinese person

SAM'S LEI SHOP

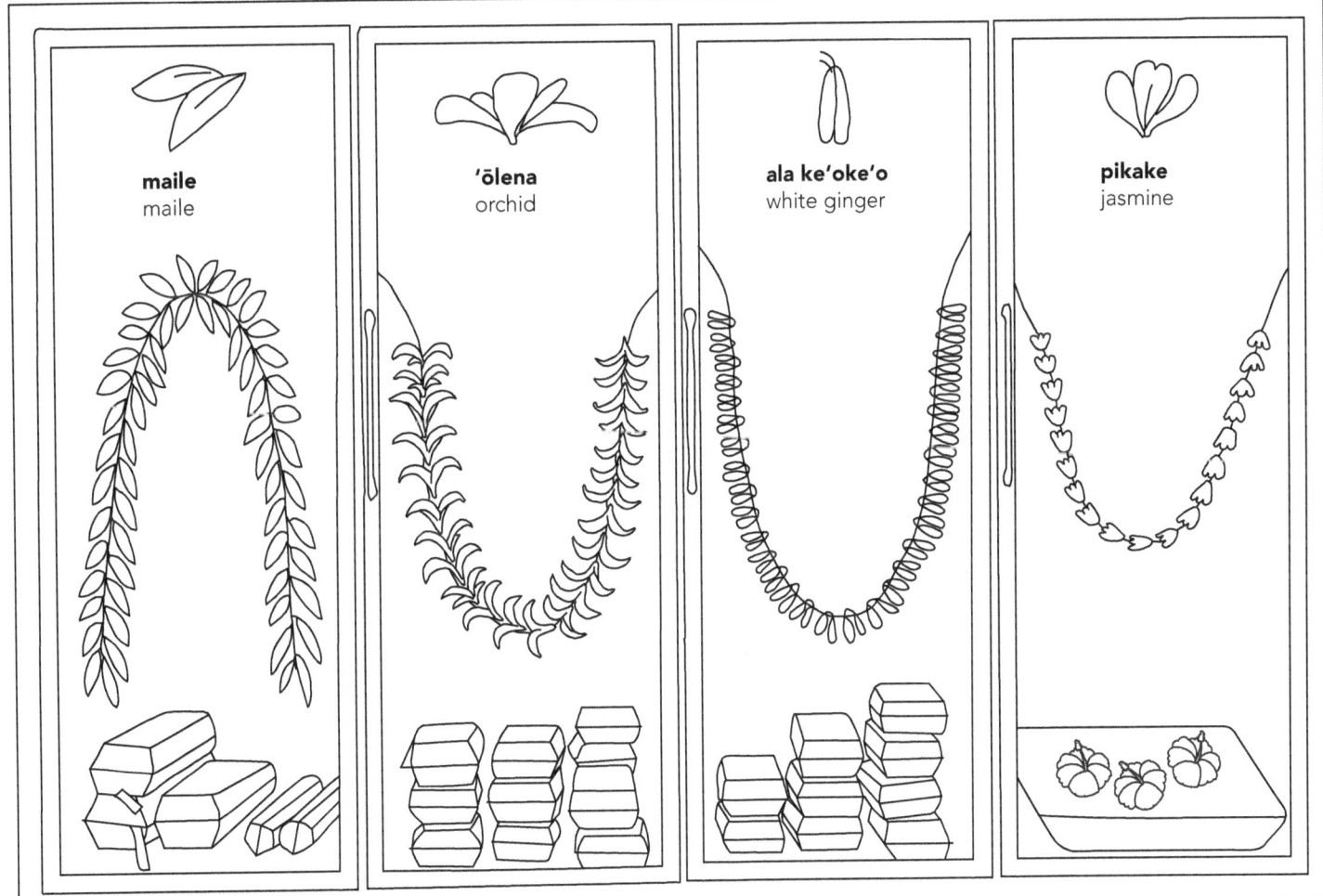

maile
maile

'ōlena
orchid

ala ke'oke'o
white ginger

pikake
jasmine

HEATHER BROWN ART
@ NORTH SHORE (Hale'iwa) & WAIKIKI

One of my favorite artists is Heather Brown, who paints colorful scenes of Hawaii that look like shimmering panes of stained glass. Her paintings are fun, whimsical, bright, and uplifting. These **nani** waves, beaches, rainbows, and tropical plants are full of color and will inspire your coloring. In fact, they inspired this book! When I was younger, my parents bought this painting called "Island View". It has three islands, representing the three people in our family! You can find Heather's original art at Wyland Galleries and her prints in many gift shops around the island. Find her at: https://heatherbrownart.com.

DON'T MISS OTHER O'AHU ART ATTRACTIONS

Honolulu Museum of Art (downtown)
Hawaii's main art museum is best known for its Hawaiian and Asian art. Come see Japanese woodblock prints, Georgia O'Keeffe's Hawaii paintings, and royal capes (yes, like Batman's) made from thousands of colorful feathers.

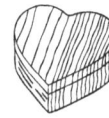

Nohea Gallery (Kahala)
My favorite art gallery features original art from local artists like Rosalie Prussing and Russell Lowrey as well as other beautiful items like koa wood jewelry boxes.

Hale'iwa galleries and shops (North Shore)
This art hot spot offers anything from fine art like Heather's (Wyland) to local artist prints (Polu Gallery) to sea glass and seashells.

Kaka'ako street art (downtown)
Kaka'ako's annual POW WOW festival leaves behind colorful street art on its walls that you can enjoy all year round. My favorite is "Aloha Monsters".

LEARN HAWAIIAN
nani *(NAH-nee)* – beautiful

IOLANI PALACE
@ DOWNTOWN HONOLULU

Iolani Palace is the only royal palace on U.S. soil. The palace for was home to Hawaiian kings, queens, and other high **ali'i** until American sugar plantation owners (with the support of local U.S. representatives but not the U.S. President) decided to force Liliuokalani, Hawai'i's last queen, to give up her throne (see O'ahu Island Insights - History to learn why). It's sad to know that this palace became the jail for Queen Liliuokalani. Some say the huge sums of money spent on the palace contributed to the overthrow of the queen. Today, you can observe the extravagance in the beautiful koa wood and luxurious furniture. Most interesting to me, the palace has indoor plumbing and electric lights, which even the White House didn't have at the time!

DON'T MISS NEARBY

Queen Emma Summer Palace
For more royal magic, visit this summer home away from the hustle and bustle. You can see the crib of Prince Albert, who would have been Kamehameha V if he hadn't passed away at age 4.

King Kamehameha statue
Just across the street from the palace, this picturesque spot makes a beautiful backdrop. Visit on June 11 to see it draped in flowers for Kamehameha Day!

Foster Botanical Garden
Walk among giant trees, exotic flowers, and hidden jungle paths in these vibrant gardens.

The Capitol Modern (formerly HiSAM)
This beautiful museum, which is free to visit, has many ancient Hawaiian-style artworks and showcases contemporary artists.

LEARN HAWAIIAN
ali'i *(ah-LEE-ee)* – chief, ruler, nobility

MAKAPU'U LIGHTHOUSE
@ WINDWARD (Makapu'u)

It can be difficult to hike under the Hawaiian sun, so try this popular trail in the evening to stay cool. The paved path is easy to hike, but if you're feeling adventurous, you can hike down the **pali** to the tidepools for a fun marine experience. Otherwise, you can continue up to the top, where you'll have a spectacular view of Makapu'u beach, the lighthouse, Rabbit Island, and the Windward coastline. On the way, you can see Koko Head Crater, the lighthouse, and even the three neighbor islands (Moloka'i, Lanai, and Maui) on a clear day. With a bit of luck, during the winter, you might even be able to spot some humpback whales!

LEARN HAWAIIAN
pali *(PAH-lee)* – cliff

DON'T MISS NEARBY

Humpback whales
These gentle giants swim to warm Hawaiian waters to have their young, and you might be able to spot them spouting or breaching through the trail's binoculars. Can you believe whales' ancestors were hippos?

Tide pools
Clamber down from the whale lookout to the tide pools, where you can swim or enjoy watching the marine wildlife.

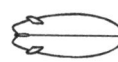

Surfers
Watch people surf from the view point at the end of the trail, or drive on to Sandy Beach, a local surfers' favorite.

Halona Blowhole & Cove
It looks like a whale spouting when the tide rushes through it! Next to the blowhole is a cove that was made famous in *From Here to Eternity*. Be careful on your way down!

Food recommendation
Try Ono Seafood in Kalama Valley, a yummy poke place that has another branch on Kapahulu Ave (see page 42).

PEARL HARBOR
@ EWA (Pearl City)

I love picking pearls from live oysters in O'ahu's jewelry stores. Did you know that Pearl Harbor got its name from the pearl oysters that used to grow there? Today, Pearl Harbor is known for being the site where World War II started for the United States. The iconic U.S.S. Arizona Memorial sits on top of the sunken battleship U.S.S. Arizona, which amazingly leaks drops of oil every day, over fifty years later. Some people call these drops black tears because of the 1,177 American sailors who died below on December 7, 1941. We say **mahalo** for their service. At Pearl Harbor, you can also see where the war ended. The peace agreement was signed on the battleship U.S.S. Missouri in Tokyo Bay on September 12, 1945, and it's now parked in Pearl Harbor.

LEARN HAWAIIAN
mahalo (*mah-HAH-loh*) – thank you

VISITING TIPS

Logistics
To avoid disappointment, reserve a ticket at Recreation.gov or pay for a tour that includes a ticket. Try leaving your bag behind to avoid the bag check line.

U.S.S. Missouri
I think it's exciting to see the place where a huge world war ended. There's a copy of the peace treaty and photos of it getting signed. Go below for interesting exhibits and some air conditioning!

Pearl Harbor Aviation Museum
Here, you'll get a chanceto immerse yourself in history! Not only will you see WWII aircraft but also 70+ year-old bullet holes from December 1941. Newer planes like an F-14 and a Blue Angel are also here.

Food recommendation
Visit Tanioka's not for the ambience but for some of the most authentic local food on O'ahu, including poke, SPAM musubi, and fried rice.

POLYNESIAN CULTURAL CENTER
@ NORTH SHORE (Laie)

I've always been curious about the Polynesian Cultural Center (PCC), which is a mini theme park covering Polynesian culture from Hawai'i, New Zealand, Samoa, Tahiti, Tonga, and Fiji. At PCC, you'll be able to learn about all sorts of interesting things like Hawaiian mythology, tiki carving, and stick games from New Zealand. Did you know that Polynesians could navigate long distances in the ocean, all without maps and compasses? They were also masters at using every part of plants like coconuts, kukui nuts, and breadfruit trees. I love my hat woven from coconut leaves that a **kama'aina** made for me at a local farmers market!

LEARN HAWAIIAN
kama'āina *(kah-mah-AH-ee-nah)* – local

DON'T MISS NEARBY

The Crouching Lions
The difficult hike to this rock formation is indefinitely closed and not maintained. It features views of Kahana Bay and the "crouching rock lion". There's also a restaurant named after the lion, which is a good choice for a sit-down meal with a nice view.

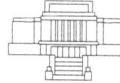

Laie Latter Day Saint Temple
The PCC is run by Mormons, so the fifth oldest Mormon church in the world is right next door. With a lush garden and reflecting pools, it's a relaxing oasis.

Outdoor Fun
There's something for everyone at the North Shore, including ziplining (Keana Ranch), horseback riding (Gunstock Ranch), and UTVs (Kualoa Ranch).

Food recommendations
The Country Eatery & Juicery is a refreshing pit stop for picking up a smoothie. Or make your way to the Kahuku Sugar Mill for even more options.

ROYAL HAWAIIAN
@ WAIKIKI

The Royal Hawaiian is my favorite hotel on O'ahu. I love its pink bathrobes, its beautiful views, and best of all, its prime location on Waikiki beach. I've spent hours building **nui** forts on the Waikiki sand. When I was younger, the hotel even let me ride on the ATV that the hotel uses to clear away all the beach gear. This hotel was built by a cruise line called Matson in 1927 to offer their passengers a luxury destination (when most people traveled here by boat). Although the hotel has a lot of history, my favorite part about it is its unique Moorish architecture (from North Africa), which makes it really stand out and suits its nickname, the "Pink Palace."

LEARN HAWAIIAN
nui *(NOO-ee)* – large

DON'T MISS WHILE YOU'RE THERE

Sheraton Waikiki's water slide
Next door at the Sheraton, it's the most fun you can have in Waikiki outside the ocean, although the Hilton, Ritz Carlton, and Aulani have slides too.

Newt at the Royal
A fanciful hat store with a long list of celebrity clients. You should at least try on some hats here, especially their panama hats.

Sand castles
Build your own Iolani Palace with easy-to-dig Waikiki sand that can support giant forts. Did you know that Waikiki's beach is quickly disappearing? They import sand from elsewhere to keep up!

Urban wildlife
There's a family of ducks that live near the lobby, and the koi pond at the Sheraton is fun to watch during feeding times.

Island Vintage Shave Ice
My favorite shave ice spot. They have lots of flavors but my favorite is strawberry and mango with mochi.

Royal Hawaiian

FOOD TRUCK PARK
@ NORTH SHORE (Hale'iwa)

Food on O'ahu is just like its people: a melting pot. You'll find plenty of Filipino, Chinese, Japanese, Korean, and Vietnamese food to accompany their large local populations, not to mention fusion dishes like SPAM musubi, poke bowls, and mochiko chicken. One of the best food truck spots is in Hale'iwa, anchored by the delicious Giovanni's shrimp truck, where they serve butter and garlic with a side of shrimp! Kaimana Shave Ice is nearby to wash it all down. Shrimp trucks are everywhere, but save up for Giovanni's or Fumi's (Ala Moana Shopping Center). Enjoy a **lu'au** every day by visiting one of the many food trucks, food halls, and foodie hotspots like Chinatown.

DON'T MISS OTHER FOOD MARKETS

Makai Market (Ala Moana)
Hawai'i's oldest and (in my opinon) best food court with lots of great choices. Try Poi Bowl for authentic and delicious Hawaiian food.

Kūhiō Ave. Food Hall (Waikiki)
Places come and go, but there's always something yummy to discover here.

Kahuku Sugar Mill (Kahuku)
This sugar mill closed 50 years ago, but now it's surrounded by food trucks and trendy shops. I like to stop to get a smoothie here!

Eat the Street (rotating)
A monthly gathering of about 40 food trucks. You'll be hard-pressed to find a bigger variety of food anywhere else!

Farmers markets (various)
Many of the larger farmers markets are a spectacle with so many different kinds of foods to try. Don't miss KCC Farmers' Market and Honolulu Farmers' Market.

LEARN HAWAIIAN
lū'au (*LOO-ow*) – Hawaiian feast

HONOLULU COOKIE COMPANY
@ HONOLULU (Sand Island) & WAIKIKI

Macadamia shortbread cookies are popular in Hawai'i because they are sturdy enough to survive the flight home, and nutty macadamia is a perfect complement to the butter. Honolulu Cookie Company's shortbread cookies are in my opinion the best in the world. Maybe it's because of their secret ingredient, macadamia nuts? They come in a variety of delicious island flavors like guava (my favorite) and mango as well as chocolate chip. They are shaped like pineapples, which are the Hawaiian symbol of hospitality. Their stores are a coloring dream with boxes in all shapes and colors. Best of all, they serve free samples, and if you get lucky, they sometimes give **keiki** a whole cookie to try.

LEARN HAWAIIAN
keiki (KAY-kee) – kid

DON'T MISS OTHER LOCAL TREATS

Mochi (in all varieties)
A chewy, rice-based dessert. Plain mochi, butter mochi, and my favorite: mochi ice cream from Bubbies, which started in Hawai'i!

Malasadas
Plain or filled with a yummy surprise, it's the ultimate Hawaiian pastry. Get them while they're hot!

Uncle's ice cream sandwiches
Try the lilikoi AKA passionfruit!

Haupia
A coconut pudding, made especially yummy using real coconut. Helena's has the best.

Chocolate covered macadamia nuts
Hawaiian Sun dark chocolate is my pick.

Maui onion chips
Frito-Lay only makes these in Hawai'i!

Arare (AKA kakimochi or rice crackers)
I especially love arare wrapped in seaweed.

ISLAND VINTAGE SHAVE ICE
@ WAIKIKI

Don't call it shaved ice, or else locals will know you're a tourist—in the local pidgin English it's called shave ice. It's hard to find Hawaiian-style shave ice on the mainland, so be sure to try this delicious treat while you're on the island. Shave ice, which originally arrived with Japanese plantation workers, is so important! It'll cool you down and turn your frown upside down. They actually make it by shaving ice off a huge block with a sharp blade, which makes it different from the crushed ice of a snow cone. That's what makes it melt in your mouth and so **'ono**. Learn to love extra ingredients that locals add, including my favorites: ice cream, strawberries, and mochi balls.

DON'T MISS MY FAVORITE SHAVE ICE PLACES ON O'AHU

Island Vintage Shave Ice (Waikiki)
Their **keiki** shave ice comes in a fun dolphin-shaped bowl. Lots of tropical flavors and added goodies like mochi!

Waiola (Kapahulu, near Waikiki)
The ice is cut so thin here that afterwards you'll truly know the difference between shave ice and snow cones.

Ice Garden (Aiea, near Pearl Harbor)
Unique toppings like pudding and beans showcase the Taiwanese flavor. A true gem.

Uncle Clay's House of Pure Aloha
(permanently closed)
My favorite shave ice place closed, but look for its pop-up offspring like Shred Shave Ice and Little HOPA.

LEARN HAWAIIAN
'ono *(OH-noh)* – yummy

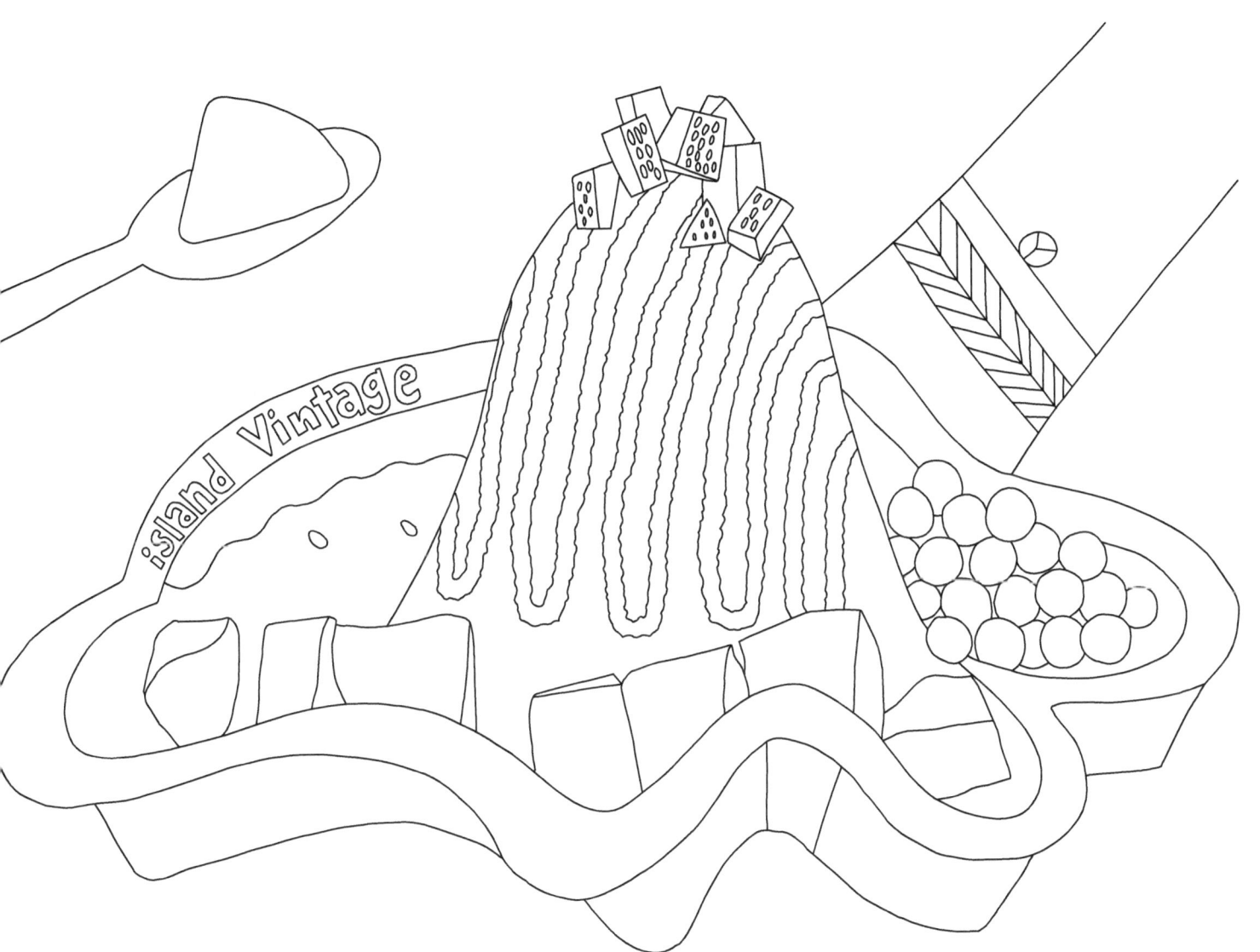

KAY'S CRACKSEED
@ HONOLULU (Manoa)

Crackseed stores are like living museums showing Hawai'i's immigrant cultures' flavors. You'll find hundreds of snacks like rice crackers, candy, shave ice, popcorn, and slushies. Locals have **hau'oli** memories of buying their favorite after school snacks. Many jars contain li hing mui (LEE-hing-moy), which is a salted plum preserved with a powder made from the skin of dried plums that captures sweet, salty, and sour flavors. Add ginger, lemon, mango varieties and options like wet or dry and seeded or seedless, then you'll understand why there are so many jars. Eat the most sour one without making a face to prove you're a local!

DON'T MISS OUR FAVORITE CRACKSEED STORES

Kay's Crackseed (Manoa)
My dad's local crackseed store, featuring Waiola-branded shave ice! His favorites include candied ginger, kakimochi, and li hing mui lemon peels.

Crack Seed Store (Kaimuki)
A true classic neighborhood crackseed store with its straightforward name could be in any local neighborhood.

Rainbow Crack Seed (Kaneohe)
Try their hurricane popcorn, which is mixed with furikake for a delicious savory treat.

Long's (many neighborhoods)
This pharmacy is now owned by CVS, but they've still kept their local touch. Shop their snack aisle for easy access to crackseed store treats including my favorite, li hing sour lychee.

LEARN HAWAIIAN
hau'oli *(how-OH-lee)* – happy

NICO'S FISH MARKET
@ HONOLULU (Downtown)

To avoid misunderstandings, pronounce this word *POH-keh*, not *pohk*. Poke or raw diced fish (or other seafood) served with seasoning, is not my favorite, but my parents like this **pūpū**. Poke bowls are a fusion creation and have spread around the world, but you'll probably find that local poke is different from back on the mainland. You'll find ingredients you can't find elsewhere like local seaweed, kukui nuts, and all different kinds of seafood, not to mention fewer non-native ingredients like corn and edamame. Poke is an authentic, ancient Hawaiian food, and the deep sea fish used to be reserved for royalty. Today, you can easily find it in local supermarkets like Foodland.

DON'T MISS OUR FAVORITE POKE PLACES

Nico's Fish Market (Downtown)
This fish market offers some of the best poke on the island.

Island Vintage Wine Bar (Waikiki)
They're known for acai bowls and coffee, but their poke bowls pack in ground kukui nut and local seaweed for an authentic taste.

Tamashiro Market (Kapālama)
Get your poke where the locals do. Find fish here you won't find anywhere else like lomi oio.

Fresh Catch (Kaneohe)
Is it so fresh because they sell so much or is it so fresh that it attracts so many people? The chicken or egg?

Ono Seafood (Kapahulu)
Be prepared to brave long lines at this local hotspot, where you order poke by the pound.

LEARN HAWAIIAN
pūpū *(POO-poo)* – appetizer

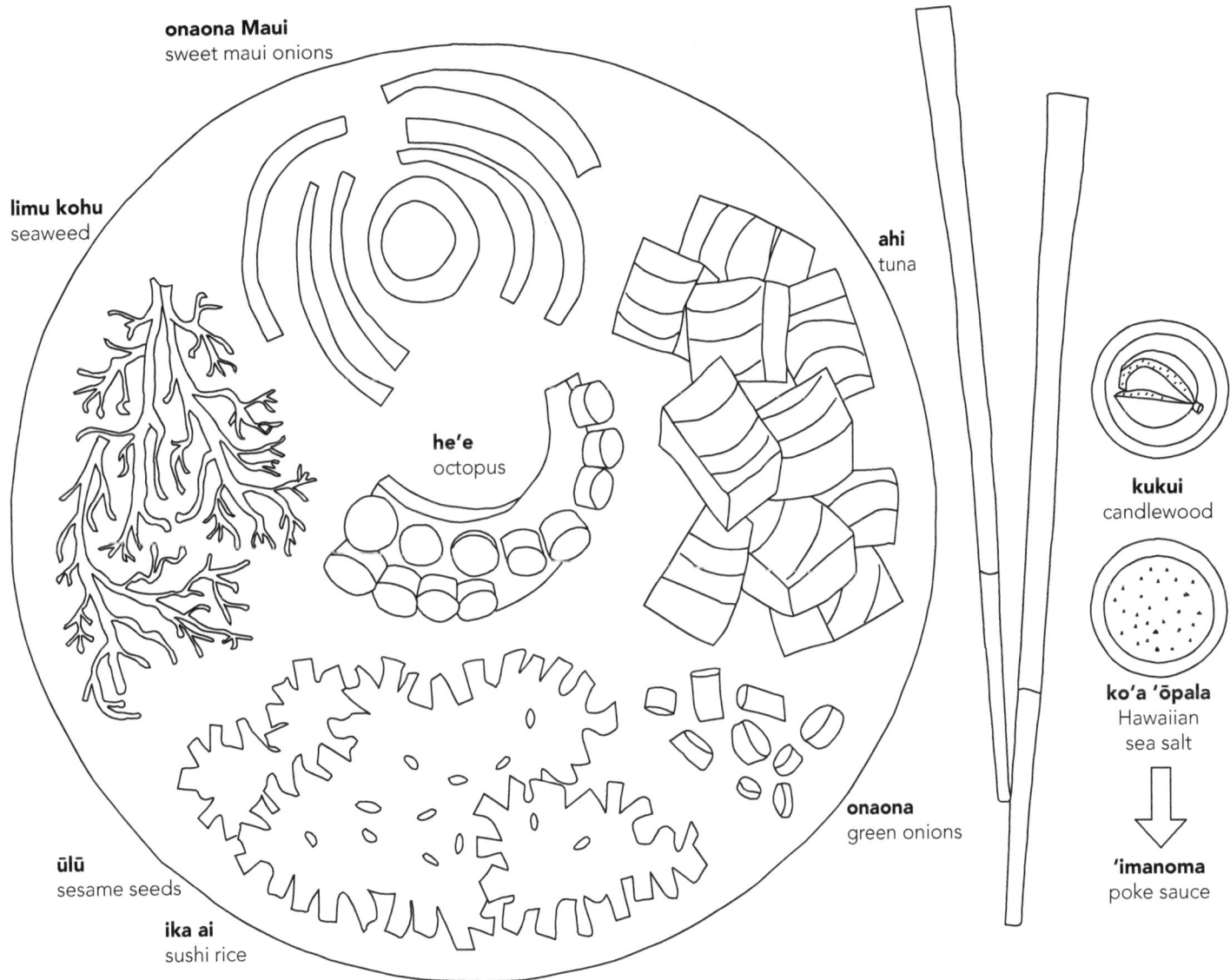

onaona Maui
sweet maui onions

limu kohu
seaweed

ahi
tuna

he'e
octopus

kukui
candlewood

ko'a 'ōpala
Hawaiian
sea salt

'imanoma
poke sauce

onaona
green onions

ūlū
sesame seeds

ika ai
sushi rice

YANAGI SUSHI
@ HONOLULU (Ala Moana)

Japanese food is great on O'ahu, thanks to flight times to Hawai'i for Japanese visitors being just two hours longer than those from California, plus a local population of Japanese ancestry that numbers about 20%. One of my favorite foods is sushi, and when you combine fresh fish daily with discerning Japanese eaters, you are guaranteed to find amazing sushi like fatty **'ahi**! My favorite sushi place in the world is Yanagi Sushi, where you will find a wonderful mix of local families, business lunchers, and celebrity diners.

DON'T MISS THESE STRAIGHT-FROM-JAPAN RESTAURANTS

Totoya (Kaimuki)
This hole-in-the-wall serves gobs of fresh seafood on rice, just like what I ate on my trip to Hokkaido. Line up early with the locals.

Ginza Bairin (Waikiki)
Featuring 100-year-old Tonkatsu recipes, this restaurant is a favorite with young and old. Make reservations to save yourself a long wait.

Katsumidori Sushi (Ala Moana)
This sushi restaurant offers fresh, premium sushi at reasonable prices, just like you might find in Tokyo.

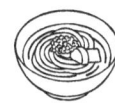

TsuruTonTan Udon Noodle (Waikiki)
Serves my favorite kind of noodles, udon, with so many choices of toppings, including salmon eggs.

LEARN HAWAIIAN
'ahi *(AH-hee)* – tuna

CHINAMAN'S HAT
@ WINDWARD (Kualoa)

Mokoli'i Islet is better known as Chinaman's island because it looks like a triangular hat that's used by some Asian farmers. Mokoli'i translates to "little **moku**", and it's the top of an old volcanic formation. To snap a nice picture of the island, you can visit Kualoa Beach Park (I call it Chicken Park because there are so many chickens), which also has a nice beach. While Chinaman's Hat is best known for its iconic shape, there are tours that will take you to visit the island by kayak and hike up to the top of the island for a beautiful view of the Ko'olau mountains!

DON'T MISS NEARBY

Royal Fish Ponds
Kualoa Ranch is next to Chinaman's Hat, and within the ranch are the royal fish ponds, which are over one thousand years old and still in use!

Secret Island Beach
Kualoa Ranch also runs tours to its secluded secret beach. You'll have the whole beach to yourself because it's only accessible by boat.

Kahana Bay
Nearby is an off-the-tourist-map beach park that was a vacation spot for royalty. Today Kahana Bay offers many choices of activities such as hiking, kayaking, fishing, and more.

Food recommendation
Waiahole Poi Factory is the perfect stop on this side of the island to fill your belly with authentic Hawaiian food like kalua pig and haupia ice cream.

LEARN HAWAIIAN
moku *(MOH-koo)* – island

DIAMOND HEAD
@ EAST HONOLULU (Diamond Head)

Diamond Head is more than just a beautiful backdrop—it's a small volcano made from ash that's not big enough to be called **mauna** (see O'ahu Island Insights on page 74 to learn more). You might be tempted to picture a diamond shape when looking at the crater, but British sailors named it Diamond Head because of the crystals they saw in the crater (they weren't diamonds, unfortunately). Native Hawaiians called it Leahi (Tuna Ridge) because the crater's shape resembles a tuna's fin. Try hiking Diamond Head, where you'll go through a dark tunnel, climb three sets of long stairs, and come out of a pillbox bunker to find the best views of Honolulu. But prepare water and sun protection—last time I was here, a helicopter came to rescue someone!

DON'T MISS NEARBY

KCC farmers' market
The largest farmer's market on the island with every local food you can imagine!

Kapahulu Avenue
A foodie heaven including Leonard's for yummy malasadas (Portuguese doughnuts), Ono for poke, Waiola's for shave ice, Side Street Inn for local favorites, and Rainbow Drive Inn for plate lunches.

Cromwell's Beach
A hidden local beach away from the tourists that has good snorkeling spots and crystal-clear water.

Shangri-La
Millionaire heiress Doris Duke's mansion-turned-museum, this place is full of beautiful Islamic art. Reservation required!

LEARN HAWAIIAN
mauna *(MAH-oo-nah)* – mountain

HANAUMA BAY
@ EAST HONOLULU (Koko Head)

Since no one is allowed to fish here, wildlife swims as if people hadn't arrived on the island yet. Last time we visited Hanauma Bay, a friendly Hawaiian monk seal even crawled onto the beach to say hello! In the water, you'll probably spot my favorites: humuhumunukunukuapua'a (which translates as "triggerfish with a snout like a pig") and uhu (parrotfish), which looks exactly as it sounds—colorful and with a beak just like a parrot. Nearby is the infamous "Toilet Bowl," a lava formation that flushes when the waves go out. Please **kōkua** and stay away—the Toilet Bowl is now closed because of some unfortunate accidents. If you're curious, see it in action on the Internet:

LEARN HAWAIIAN
kōkua *(koh-KOO-ah)* – cooperate

VISITING TIPS

Reservations!
Make reservations at least two days ahead at 7:00 AM to avoid disappointment. Walk-ins are possible before 1:30 PM, so show up early if you didn't reserve a spot, but remember that it's closed on Mondays and Tuesdays.

Protect Wildlife
Avoid stepping on any coral; they are living beings and home to wildlife. The reef will appreciate your reef-safe sunscreen.

Sun protection
There's not much shade, so bring sunscreen or a hat to have a better experience while you're here and no sunburn afterwards!

Rodents
Beware the mongooses, who will boldly steal your food!

Food recommendation
There is a concession stand at the top after you enter the park, but bring your own packed food to save yourself a hike. Hanapa'a Market nearby has good plate lunches.

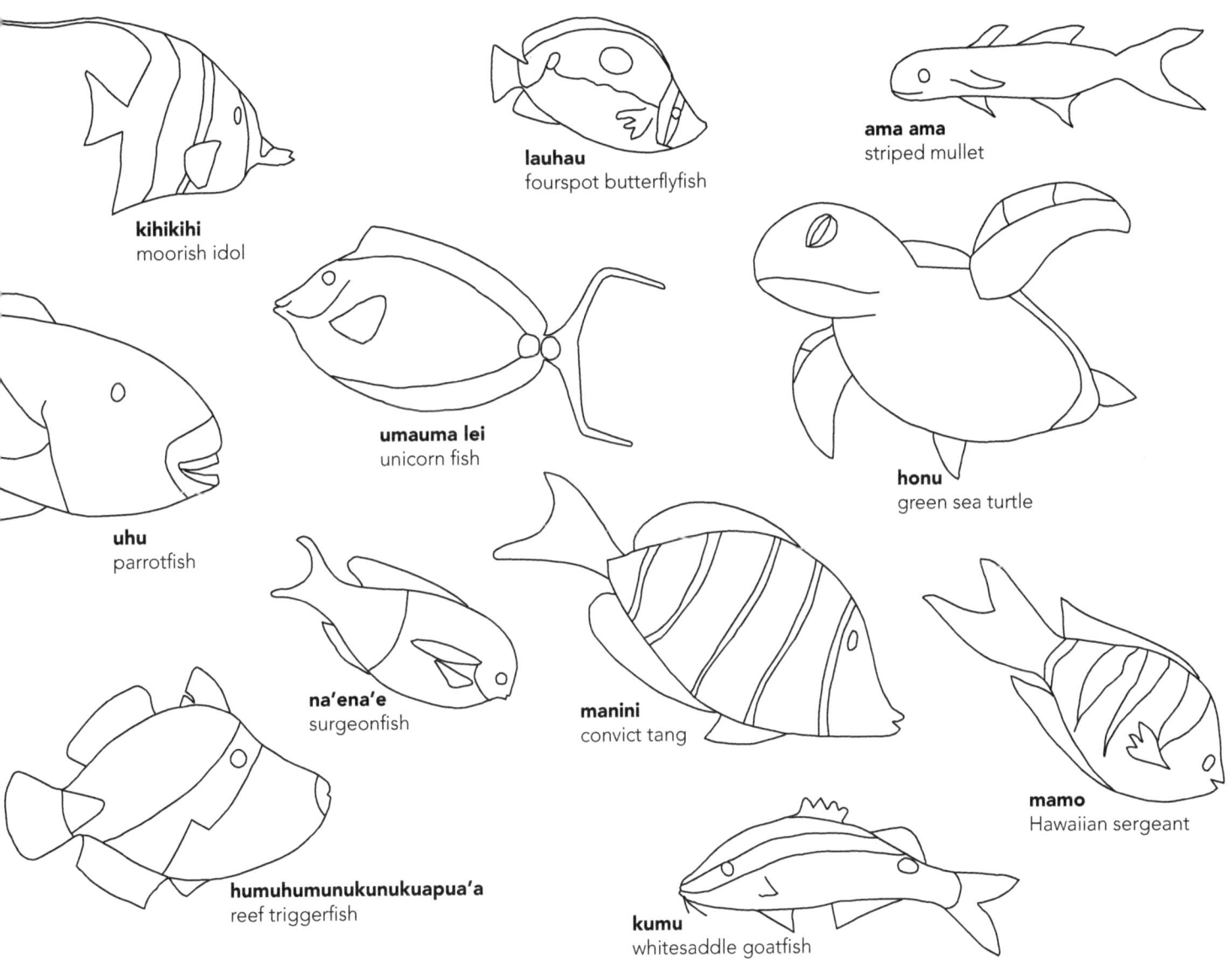

kihikihi
moorish idol

lauhau
fourspot butterflyfish

ama ama
striped mullet

uhu
parrotfish

umauma lei
unicorn fish

honu
green sea turtle

na'ena'e
surgeonfish

manini
convict tang

mamo
Hawaiian sergeant

humuhumunukunukuapua'a
reef triggerfish

kumu
whitesaddle goatfish

45

KO OLINA LAGOONS
@ EWA (Kapolei)

Ko Olina has some amazing lagoons that are safe for swimming and feature a variety of wildlife. Did you know that the lagoons were manmade in the 1970s to support the tourist industry? This area is similar to the Big Island or Maui resorts, but only here will you find Aulani, Disney's Hawaii resort. Ko Olina is only half-built, so the next time you come, there might be another resort **makai**, like the first Atlantis resort in the U.S.! Last time I was at Ko Olina, I saw lots of fish that I wanted to catch. We didn't bring a net, so we used my aunt's hat to catch a couple of minnows!

DON'T MISS NEARBY

Pink Pillbox hike (at sunset)
Known officially as the Pu'u O Hulu trail, this is a moderate 1.6 mile roundtrip hike. Try a sunset hike to enjoy the west-facing view of the ocean and Waianae mountains in the background.

Electric Beach
For strong swimmers only, consider a snorkeling trip to this beach. It's next to a power plant that pumps out warm water, which attracts dolphins and beautiful fish.

Ko Olina Secret Lagoon
This natural lagoon between the Four Seasons and Paradise Cove Luau features good snorkeling.

Food recommendations
Ko Olina is a bit of a dry patch outside of the resorts, but the popular Monkeypod Kitchen has a lively atmosphere, and for real local food, try Broke da Mouth Grindz in Kapolei.

LEARN HAWAIIAN
makai (ma-KAI) – toward the sea

LANIKAI BEACH
@ WINDWARD (Kailua)

You might think of Lanikai Beach when you picture a perfect Hawaiian beach. After all, "Lani **kai**" means heavenly sea, and its powdery sand, views of the two Mokulua islands, and range of fun activities make it a favorite with tourists and locals. Local shops rent out gear for snorkeling, fishing, boogie boarding, canoeing, and more. You can even kayak to the bigger island, Moku Nui, or walk to the nearby Pillbox hiking trail to the old World War II bunkers above, where you can get picture-perfect views of Lanikai. I love to build sand castles here and then take a plunge in the sparkling waves to cool down. I really wish I could bring my dog here to run around on the beach!

LEARN HAWAIIAN
kai *(KAI)* – seaside, sea, sea water, tide

VISITING TIPS

Be early
There is limited parking and it's a popular beach! It might be worth it to go for an early visit to enjoy the sunrise from the beach or hiking trail.

Portuguese men-of-war
Beware of these small blue jellyfish-like creatures that wash up on shore, their long stingers hurt a lot!

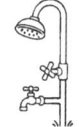

Facilities at Kailua Beach Park
You could walk from Kailua Beach Park—a 15-20-minute walk away, with good options for parking, restrooms, or rinsing off. If you find parking in Lanikai, bring a big jug of water to rinse off (there are no showers here!)

Food recommendations
The iconic Kalapawai Market is nearby if you want to picnic. If you're looking for great seafood, check out Paia Fish Market. Also save time for Manoa Chocolate's Tasting Room, where you can sample their great flavors.

NORTH SHORE WAVES
@ NORTH SHORE (Hale'iwa)

Oahu's North Shore is famous for big wave surfing, especially at the Banzai Pipeline, where the waves form a perfect tube for surfers to ride. These **nalu** make for some amazing photos with surfers in the "green room" of blue-green glass, completely surrounded by the water from the big waves. Waves here are biggest during winter, when winter storms combine with natural wind patterns and the North Shore's unique reef drop-off to make the biggest waves in Hawai'i. I've tried surfing, but I'm *definitely* not ready to surf here!

SURFING TIPS

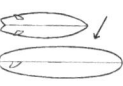

Use a longboard
Larger boards are more steady, so you won't be falling as much. Soft-top foam boards are also more forgiving and hurt less if you fall.

Look to where you want to go
If you focus on stable objects far away like the beach or buildings, it'll be much easier to keep your balance because you'll know which way is up.

Keep your knees bent and weight low
It's easier to keep your balance when you're not standing upright.

Learn to read waves
It's much easier to catch just-breaking waves than unbroken ones. They will take you along with them!

LEARN HAWAIIAN
nalu *(NAH-loo)* – waves

SHARK'S COVE
@ NORTH SHORE (Pūpūkea)

Shark's Cove, whose name comes from the shark-like shape of the rock formation when seen from above, not from the **manō** in the water. I love to snorkel in Kapo'o Tidepool, which is next to Shark's Cove. The tidepool is like a large swimming pool, except filled with colorful fish! But you might see a white-tip reef shark here along with all kinds of colorful fish. Shark's Cove is a snorkeler's paradise! If you're not a snorkeler or haven't brought your gear, don't worry. You can stay in the tidepools and see plenty of fish—the tidepools have sandy bottoms and are protected from the waves, so you don't even have to get your whole body wet.

VISITING TIPS

Footwear
Bring water shoes or fins, because the bottom of Shark's Cove is covered with rocks and coral.

Avoid winter
Aim for a summer visit, when waves are calmer, so you'll have a better snorkeling experience.

Take it slow
Access to the cove might involve climbing over many rocks; if you can, enter where there is sand.

Don't touch the coral
Coral are living animals! They are home for the fish, so please keep them healthy by not touching them. They could also hurt you!

LEARN HAWAIIAN
manō (MAH-noh) – shark

TURTLE BEACH
@ NORTH SHORE (Kahuku)

Laniakea Beach is better known as Turtle Beach because you can reliably count on seeing a green sea turtle resting on the beach here. In many cultures, seeing a turtle is considered good luck, so I hope you spot a **honu** on the beach (or better yet, in the ocean) during your visit. Did you know that each turtle's shell is unique like a human fingerprint? Green sea turtles are making a comeback from the endangered species list. I've seen them while surfing in Waikiki, snorkeling in Kaneohe, and while visiting my grandparents' house. Last time we visited Turtle Beach, I saw a rare *baby* sea turtle!

VISITING TIPS

Keep your distance
Stay at least 10 feet away and never touch a turtle. It harms them plus it's illegal.

Maximize your chances
Try to visit during lunch time, when the turtles are more likely to make an appearance.

Parking
Park in the parking lot immediately to the right of the highway going north. The lot was made to reduce traffic on this road and to keep you safe when crossing the highway.

Talk to the volunteer guides
There are usually volunteers on hand to keep people away from the turtles. They are very knowledgeable about turtles, so be sure to ask them plenty of questions!

LEARN HAWAIIAN
honu *(HOH-noo)* – turtle

WAIMEA BAY
@ NORTH SHORE (Pūpūkea)

Waimea Bay is one of the most iconic North Shore spots, with St. Peter and Paul's church overlooking the small bay. During the summer the water is calm, so you can swim, snorkel, and (at your own risk) leap off "Da Big Rock" into the **moana** for a cliff-jumping adventure! During the winter, the reef near the shore makes the big waves coming from the northwest into huge waves, which is why Waimea Bay is the birthplace of big wave surfing. But be careful—last time I was here, there was an unexpectedly big wave that washed away keys, phones, and almost me!

LEARN HAWAIIAN
moana *(MOH-ah-nah)* – ocean

DON'T MISS NEARBY

Giovanni's
The original shrimp truck serves amazing shrimp scampi. The long lines will be worth it!

Shave ice institutions
Matsumoto's shave ice stand attracts a long line of devoted fans, including chickens who will ask you to share! Or try Kaimana for natural shave ice flavors.

Pillbox hike
Near the beautiful Sunset Beach is a beautiful North Shore hike to a (another) pillbox. Find parking at Sunset Elementary School.

Waimea Valley
This beautiful park features all sorts of plants along a leisurely hike to a waterfall. It might be a trickle during the dry season, though!

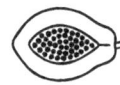

Malama Market
A local grocery store that is an oasis with local staples like poke and SPAM musubi. You might see a food tour picking out fresh local papaya to taste.

DOLE PLANTATION
@ EWA (Wahiawa)

O'ahu used to send pineapples to the rest of the world, but now the big farms are gone. At the Dole Plantation, you'll have a chance to ride the Pineapple Express train, where you'll learn all about the history of pineapples on O'ahu. **Hala kahiki** are a symbol of hospitality and were once luxury items. You'll also see pineapples growing right on small shrub-like plants—they don't grow on trees! I love pineapples, and Hawaiian pineapples are some of the sweetest in the world. Did you know that you can plant the crown (green part) from a pineapple, and it will grow a full pineapple plant? Imagine the pineapple you eat as the crown of many more generations of pineapples.

LEARN HAWAIIAN
hala kahiki *(HAH-lah kah-HEE-kee)* – pineapple

DON'T MISS OTHER LOCAL FRUITS

Mango
My favorite fruit of all time. If you find one at a farmers market, definitely try the pirie (*PIH-ree*) variety—it will blow your mind!

Passionfruit (lilikoi)
A tart fruit that I enjoy in shave ice or ice cream flavors. Also the P in POG juice.

Lychee
A delicious fruit that is like a poky red grape with a big seed. Don't forget to peel it first!

Apple Banana
These bananas are packed with more sweet flavor than any banana from home. That is, unless you're from Central America!

Guava
If strawberry guavas are in season look for them next to the trail during your hike for a delicious snack!

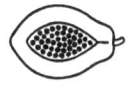

Papaya
A large orange fruit with a softer, milder taste than mangos.

Coconut
The star of Hawaiian desserts, they also offer a refreshing drink on hot days.

FIREWORKS AT THE HILTON
@ WAIKIKI

The Hilton Hawaiian Village is an enormous resort that features fireworks every Friday night. The **ho'olaule'a** takes place right next to the Hilton's saltwater lagoon, which is packed with fish and worth a visit just to chase those fish down and play in the water. Their water slide is in the nearby pool, but be prepared for long lines. Before and after the show, the surrounding area is a bustling place with all sorts of light-up toys for sale, so it's a whole lot of fun. If you stay at the Hilton, you get your own special viewing area near the pool, but be sure to line up early.

DON'T MISS OTHER KID-FRIENDLY WAIKIKI ACTIVITIES

Honolulu Zoo
Spot the state bird (nene) here, along with flamingos, giraffes, and zebras.

Waikiki Aquarium
See all the fish that you couldn't spot while snorkeling!

Atlantis Submarine
Dive into the water off Waikiki to observe marine life, coral reefs, and sunken ships, all without getting wet...need I say more?

Duke's Lane
I love shopping here for trinkets from the local kiosks. A perfect place to pick up souvenirs; This is what Waikiki used to be like.

Sunset Stories Hula Show
A rare free show in Waikiki at the International Marketplace, come here to learn about Hawaiian culture.

LEARN HAWAIIAN
ho'olaule'a *(hoh-oh-LAU-leh-ah)* – celebration

TRANSPORTATION
@ Various

There are so many different ways to get around the island, including the **Wiki Wiki** Shuttle between terminals at the airport. One of my favorites is the Waikiki Trolley, which runs both old-style trolleys and double decker buses. I love taking efficient public transportation, and one way to get around on public transit is the bus, which on O'ahu is called, well, TheBus. Did you know that in 1901, O'ahu had the first electric railway transit system in the United States? It closed in 1941, but Skyline, a new rail system, opened in 2023. To travel between islands, you'll probably fly on a Boeing 717 on one of my favorite airlines, Hawaiian! Many years ago, there was a high-speed ferry, but it was dangerous to local wildlife and was shut down.

TRANSPORTATION TIPS:

Waikiki Trolley
This is Honolulu's hop-on-hop-off trolley and bus tour, perfect for convenient access to the main sites. Most of the trolleys are buses these days, but you might get lucky with a classic trolley!

HOLO Card
Get your day pass easily at any ABC Store for only $7.50 (and half-price for kids!). Use the card on buses or the Skyline.

Circle Island Tour
Hop on TheBus number 55 to circle the island all day long for a fraction of the cost of a guided tour, and all at your own pace. Buses come about every 30 minutes.

HEA-TheBus
Download the free app for real-time bus arrival information.

LEARN HAWAIIAN
wikiwiki *(WEE-kee-wee-kee)* – speedy

SEA LIFE PARK
@ WINDWARD (Waimanalo)

Sea Life Park was a pioneer in training animals like dolphins. Positive reinforcement training of **nāia** here had wide influence, even on our dog training today. It's an amazing park with birds, an aquarium, and the dolphin show, which is simply magical. You'll also see one of the world's only *wholphins* (half dolphin and half false killer whale) here. Sea Life Park is the only place where sea turtles are actively bred, and they release up to 600 into the wild every year. This is the only place on O'ahu where you're allowed to feed them! (You might recognize the park from the movie *50 First Dates*.)

DON'T MISS WHILE YOU'RE THERE

Dolphin show
Plan your visit around this show, which takes place daily at either 12:15PM or 3:30PM. These dolphins dance on water! It's a show you have to see with your own eyes to believe.

Dolphin experience
Sea Life Park is one of two places on the island where you can swim with dolphins (the other is at the Kahala Hotel). This experience is ideal for younger kids.

Turtle feeding
Get close to sea turtles here! Unlike wild turtles, you don't have to stay 10 feet away.

Bird aviary
These crazy lovebirds and cockatiels will eat right out of your hands. Last time I was here, one stood on my head to say aloha!

LEARN HAWAIIAN
nāia *(NAH-ee-ah)* – dolphin

OFFICIAL HAWAI'I STATE SYMBOLS

Surfing
(state sport)
Surfing was the sport of Hawaiian kings, but now anyone can try it. I took several surf lessons at Waikiki beach, which is my favorite beach in the world.

Shaka
(state gesture)
Shakas send good vibes and can mean thank you, hang loose, stay cool, and other ways to say aloha. In 2024, the state legislature made it the official state gesture of Hawai'i!

Hula
(state dance)
Hawai'i's state dance is most often seen as luau entertainment. Each motion of the hands or hips signifies a specific word in a story or chant.

Kukui
(state tree)
Kukui trees have nuts that are fun to craft into things like bracelets and leis. They are also called candlenut, because Native Hawaiians used oil from the nuts as candles!

Humuhumunukunukuapua'a
(hoo-moo-hoo-moo-NU-koo-noo-koo-ah-poo-ah-ah)
(state fish)
A fish whose name is fun to say, and better yet, you might see them if you go snorkeling. They are easy to spot because of their unique and colorful pattern!

Nēnē
(state bird)
These geese arrived from Canada 500,000 years ago, long before people arrived). They're an endangered species, so you probably won't see one unless you go to the Big Island or visit the zoo.

Flag
(state flag)
Hawai'i's flag features eight stripes, one for each of the main Hawaiian islands and a Union Jack, because of the historical alliance between the Hawaiian kingdom and Britain.

Yellow Hibiscus
(state flower)
Hibiscus can be used in many useful ways—in drinks, food, medicine, skincare, and more! Ancient Hawaiian women put them over their ear to signal whether they were married or single.

Ukulele
(state instrument)
The ukulele is like a mini guitar, except with only 4 strings instead of 6. The word ukulele roughly translates to "jumping flea," and if you see a musician playing one, you might understand why!

Surfing

Kukui

Flag

Shaka

Humuhumunukunukuapua'a

Hibiscus

Hula

Nēnē

Ukulele

UNOFFICIAL HAWAI'I ICONS

Chicken
Chickens are everywhere on O'ahu these days, thanks to escaped chickens that mixed with wild chickens. You'll have a hard time missing them!

Rainbows
These aren't unique to Hawai'i, but you'll see them often because Hawai'i's rain often coexists with sun. Locals call the rain "liquid sunshine!"

POG
Tropical flavors of passion fruit, orange, and guava come together in this delicious juice. On your flight home, ask your flight attendant for it—several airlines serve it on flights to and from Hawai'i.

SPAM
Hawai'i's unofficial food staple, SPAM is a local favorite. SPAM musubis are my go-to Hawaiian food because you can find them almost everywhere! You can also try SPAM-flavored macadamia nuts.

Banyan tree
These massive trees from India grow by sprouting new roots from their branches, growing like a web of vines. They are fun to climb!

Gecko
Hopefully you don't see them, but geckos are plentiful outdoors and will sneak indoors. They have puffy toes, which makes them different from mainland lizards.

Mango
You'll never eat a yummier mango than the pirie mangoes from O'ahu. There are 63 mango varieties in Hawai'i, many of which grow in residential areas where locals go "street shopping".

Mynah bird
These birds are everywhere and also featured in Hawaii's version of "The 12 Days of Christmas". I call them Hawaiian pigeons and they're fun to chase.

Plumeria
These flowers are beautiful and smell great. It's too bad they don't last long once picked, but they'll look great in your hair.

Answers: see our website, http://hirainbowrooster.com

Chicken

Rainbows

POG

SPAM

Banyan tree

Gecko

Mango

Mynah bird

Plumeria

MY O'AHU TRAVEL JOURNAL

I like to keep a travel journal of my vacations to help me remember my experience. Below are some of the things I like to capture. I hope you will take away some fond memories of your vacation to O'ahu.

Flying the coop

I traveled to O'ahu (circle one) *alone* or *with my* _____.

My vacation started on _____ and ended on _____.

We traveled on a _____ from _____.

The title of my vacation should be _____ _____.

My egg-cellent adventure

My favorite food was _____.

My favorite place to visit was _____.

My favorite experience was _____.

My worst experience was _____.

O'ahu has too (circle one) many/few _____.

I wish O'ahu had _____ from back home.

If I had one more day on O'ahu, I would have spent it _____.

Rooster revelations

The most interesting thing I learned about O'ahu was _____

_____.

The Hawaiian custom that I'm most likely to adopt is _____.

Happy hen or regretful rooster?

The funniest moment on my vacation was when _____

_____.

If I someone told me I had to spend the rest of my life on O'ahu, I would _____

_____.

DRAW YOUR FAVORITE MEMORY OF O'AHU

TRAVEL SCAVENGER GAME

ACTIVITY	POTENTIAL	PLAYER 1	PLAYER 2
Absorb local culture			
Learned how to say "hello" and "thank you" in Hawaiian	5 points	_____	_____
Took public transit (bus or rail)	5 points	_____	_____
Ate at a restaurant where you saw no other tourists	2 points (each)	_____	_____
Spoke to an O'ahu local (who is not in customer service)	3 points (each)	_____	_____
Received fruit from a local	5 points	_____	_____
Was invited by a local to their home or an event	10 points	_____	_____
Try new things			
Visited an attraction (egg) in this book	1 point (each)	_____	_____
Tried a new food	2 points (each)	_____	_____
Found a new food you like	5 points	_____	_____
Got lost finding something off the tourist path	5 points	_____	_____
Learn about O'ahu			
Can pronounce Hawai'i and humuhumunukunukuapu'a correctly	2 points (each)	_____	_____
Can point to Hale'iwa on a blank O'ahu map	5 points	_____	_____
Learned the words of a Hawaiian song	10 points	_____	_____
Tried hula dancing	5 points	_____	_____
Tally your score!		TOTAL _____	_____

Are you a(n)...

egg
0-10 points

chick
10-20 points

cockerel
21-30 points

rooster
31-60 points

Rainbow Rooster
>60 points

O'AHU BY THE NUMBERS

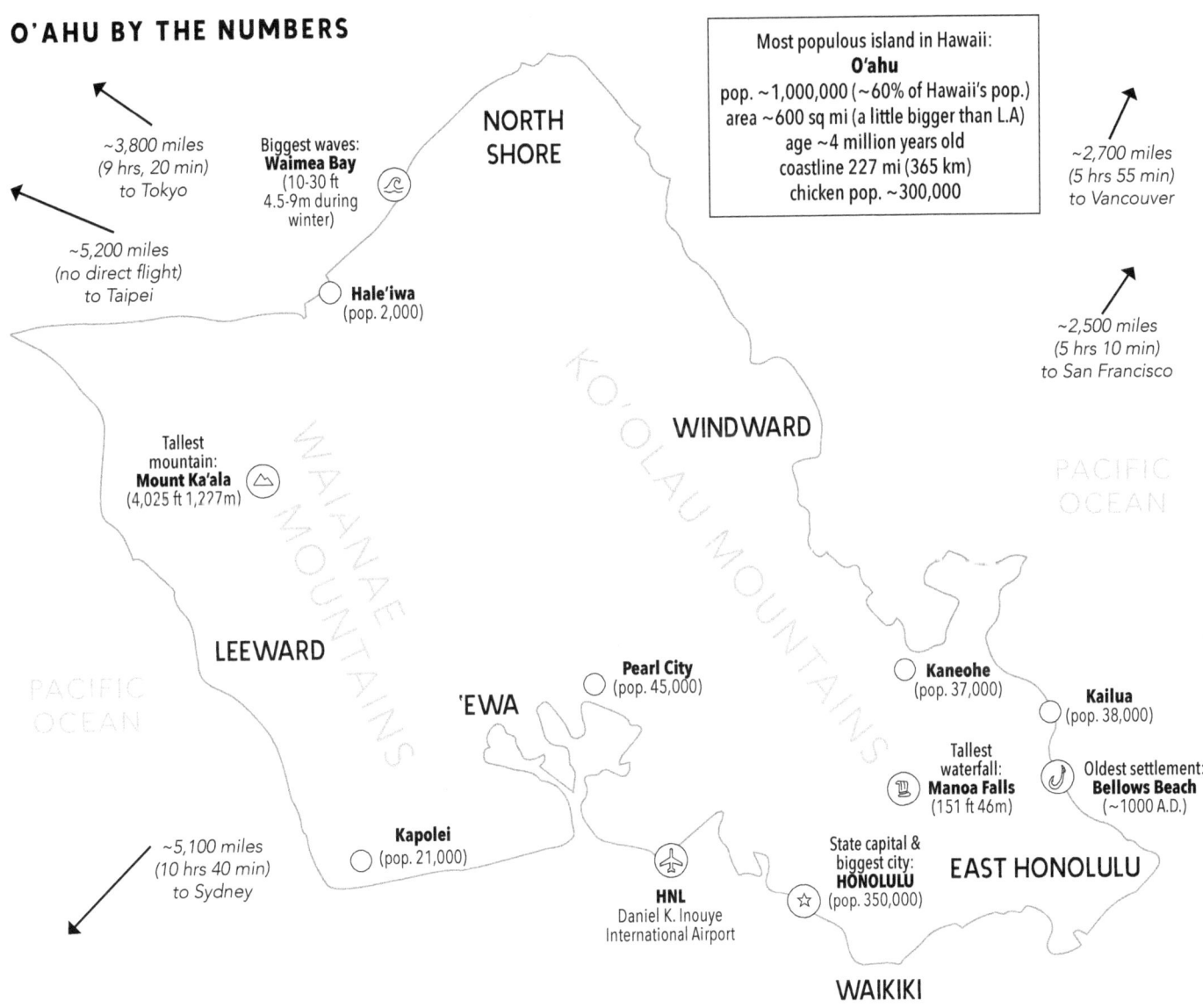

~3,800 miles
(9 hrs, 20 min)
to Tokyo

~5,200 miles
(no direct flight)
to Taipei

Biggest waves:
Waimea Bay
(10-30 ft
4.5-9m during
winter)

NORTH SHORE

Most populous island in Hawaii:
O'ahu
pop. ~1,000,000 (~60% of Hawaii's pop.)
area ~600 sq mi (a little bigger than L.A)
age ~4 million years old
coastline 227 mi (365 km)
chicken pop. ~300,000

~2,700 miles
(5 hrs 55 min)
to Vancouver

~2,500 miles
(5 hrs 10 min)
to San Francisco

Hale'iwa
(pop. 2,000)

KO'OLAU MOUNTAINS

WINDWARD

PACIFIC OCEAN

Tallest mountain:
Mount Ka'ala
(4,025 ft 1,227m)

WAIANAE MOUNTAINS

LEEWARD

'EWA

Pearl City
(pop. 45,000)

Kaneohe
(pop. 37,000)

Kailua
(pop. 38,000)

PACIFIC OCEAN

Tallest waterfall:
Manoa Falls
(151 ft 46m)

Oldest settlement:
Bellows Beach
(~1000 A.D.)

Kapolei
(pop. 21,000)

~5,100 miles
(10 hrs 40 min)
to Sydney

State capital &
biggest city:
HONOLULU
(pop. 350,000)

EAST HONOLULU

HNL
Daniel K. Inouye
International Airport

WAIKIKI

O'AHU ISLAND INSIGHTS

GEOGRAPHY

How did this island form in the middle of nowhere?

The Hawaiian islands are the most remote islands in the world, which is why your flight was so long. The nearest land is Baja California (Mexico), which is about 2,000 miles away. There are 137 islands in total but just 8 "main" islands that are the largest (and youngest!). All Hawaiian islands were made by a hole in the Pacific Plate. As the tectonic plate moves, the hole stays put and lava flows out of the hole to create a new island near the old one.

O'ahu was formed by three giant volcanoes, not two, as scientists previously thought. A mother volcano sunk into the ocean, and later two child volcanos grew on top of it. You could imagine these two volcanos growing to meet in the middle, like in the Pixar film *I Lava You*.

O'ahu is the third-oldest island out of Hawai'i's main islands. You can tell it's old by the steep faces of the mountains like the Ko'olaus, which have been carved away by rain and wind.

Why don't I see any volcanos (in the shape of a shield)?

You'll see small tuff cones (formed by ash, like Diamond Head) but no giant shield volcanoes (formed by lava). That's because over a million years ago, half of the Ko'olau shield volcano slid into the sea in one of the world's biggest-ever avalanches! It created a massive tsunami in the Pacific Ocean and left an undersea heap of land called the Tuscaloosa Seamount. The same thing happened on the other side of the island (but in slow motion, over millions of years), creating another undersea heap offshore called the Waianae Slump.

UNDERSEA IMAGE OF THE OCEAN FLOOR

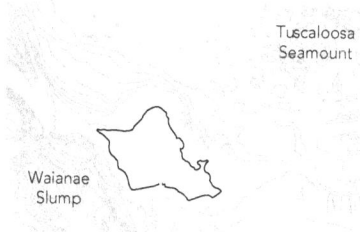

How long does it take to drive around the island?

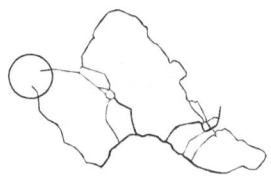

Trick question! There is (currently) no road that goes all the way around the island, thanks to a gap in the northwest caused by the Waianae mountains and the nature preserve called Kaena Point (see left). It takes about 3½ hours to drive about 100 miles around the island, taking a shortcut around the Waianae range.

If O'ahu is an island, why is there an interstate highway?

As you drive around O'ahu, you might take an interstate highway such as H-1. Hawaii interstates don't go to other islands, much less other states. Unlike other roads that are built by the local governments, these highways are funded by the federal government instead of Hawai'i, so they are still called interstate highways.

HISTORY

Who were the first people on O'ahu?
Scientists aren't sure! Analyzing differences in stories passed down, language similarities, old objects, DNA, and when dirt near ponds was disturbed, they think the first human settlements were around the year 1,000 CE, from either the Marquesan Islands or Tahiti. They cleverly brought chickens with them!

How do you become King of Hawaii?
Hawaii was ruled by local chiefs who often fought. King Kamehameha was born on the Big Island, nephew to a powerful chief. After buying guns and learning to use them from American and British traders, Kamehameha conquered the Big Island and Maui. Eventually he turned to O'ahu. In the epic Battle of Nu'uanu in 1795 (below), Kamehameha's warriors beat local forces and became Hawaii's first king. His son later moved Hawaii's capital to O'ahu, which had a natural harbor, more people, and more fertile land.

How did sugar lead to the end of the kingdom?
Over time, rich American and European sugar plantation owners became very powerful. These landowners forced the Hawaiian king to sign away some of his power in 1887. When Hawaii's queen tried to get some of it back six years later, the plantation owners forced her to step down with the help of the local American representative (even though President Cleveland opposed it). Landowners wanted Hawaii to join the U.S. so they could avoid paying tariffs.

Why was Pearl Harbor targeted during WWII?
Although Hawaii became part of the U.S. in 1898, Hawaii was not yet a state in 1941. During these 43 years, the U.S. built a very large military presence in Hawaii, including eight battleships. Because Japan wanted to expand in the Pacific, they hoped that a crushing blow at Pearl Harbor would lead the U.S. to accept Japan's control of the Pacific. Fortunately, three aircraft carriers were out to sea that morning and escaped unharmed.

Why do I see reggae-colored flags with paddles and upside-down Hawaiian flags around the island?
You'll see many of these flags in Waimanalo, where native Hawaiians were granted land by the U.S. government in 1921 and again in 2016. The Kanaka Maoli flag (left) was introduced in 2001 and today has become a symbol of native Hawaiians, many of whom dislike the U.K. and U.S. influences present in the current flag. Flying Hawaii's flag upside-down (right) means that Hawaii's status is upside down after the 1893 overthrow of the Queen—that Hawaii should once again be its own nation.

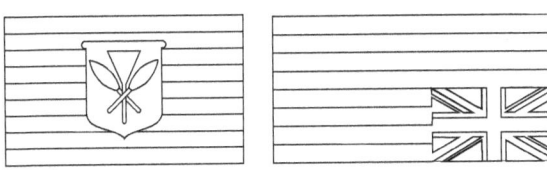

PEOPLE & CULTURE

Why is Hawai'i called the melting pot?

O'ahu embodies Hawai'i's nickname, the melting pot. People here come from all kinds of backgrounds, including from the native Hawaiian population who first inhabited Hawai'i. Here is a current picture of O'ahu's population of 1 million people:

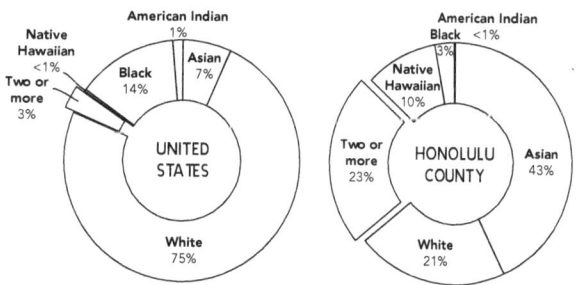

Source: State of Hawaii - Department of Business, Economic Development & Tourism

Notice that people from multi-racial backgrounds (two or more) are 23% of the population, up from 19% just 20 years ago. A true melting pot!

Wat funny kine English people stay talkin'?

You might notice some locals speaking a strange kind of English that doesn't sound familiar. That's because they are speaking Pidgin English, a more simple form of the language. Pidgin doesn't care so much about proper grammar, so it's easier to learn and understand. Pidgin even incorporates words from other languages, because of Hawaii's melting pot of immigrants who added to the language too!

Does everyone in Hawai'i surf?

When my dad first went to school in the U.S. mainland, the most common thing people asked after learning he was from Hawaii was: do you surf? Well, according to a 2000 survey by the U.S. government (NOAA), about one-third (34%) of the Hawaiian population surfs. That's over 20% of all surfers in the whole country!

What might you do to anger Hawaiian gods?

When visiting O'ahu, you might want to pay attention to local superstitions. For example, it's considered bad luck to take home sand or rocks from the beach. The fire goddess Pele will not be happy. Hawaii Volcanoes National Park receives thousands of pounds of returned rocks every year from tourists who have had a spell of bad luck. Another superstition is don't whistle at night—if you do, you might bring out little night marchers who cause mischief. On the other hand, Hawaiians think the ti plant (see left) brings good luck and will keep you safe. Look for them at sporting events!

Could you survive life in ancient Hawaii?

Ancient Hawaiian customs might seem out of place today. Women were not allowed to to eat pork, bananas, or coconuts, which were reserved for men! Some other customs are similar to today's. Instead of wearing rings, women wore flower on their right ear if they were single and on their left if they were taken.

ABOUT US

SAM CHEN (AKA Rainbow Rooster)
Author
Sam is a 10 year-old kid, who lives in Seattle and has visited Hawaii over 20 times. In his free time he likes to play soccer, eat Asian food, and take photos. His favorite things to do on O'ahu include eating shave ice, going to Waikiki Beach, visiting his grandparents' house (which you can color!) and hiking up the Ko'olau mountains.

ROBERT CHEN
Author
Robert is Sam's dad and grew up on O'ahu. He spent his mostly chicken-free youth roaming the streams of Manoa Valley in the heart of Honolulu and chasing fish in the ocean near Chinaman's hat. Robert's favorite things to do in Hawaii include kayaking to the Kaneohe sandbar, eating shave ice, and hiking up the Ko'olau mountains.

EMILY LEE
Illustrator
Emily attends high school in Monterey, California. She spends most of her time playing sports including swimming, water polo, and running. Her hobbies include reading, working out, and traveling. She is Sam's older cousin and has grown up alongside him. She specially enjoys drawing and painting, especially nature.

WAIBUN LEE
Illustrator
Waibun is Sam's uncle. He lived in Hawaii for a year when he was very young, before his family moved to Southern California. Now Carmel is his home, and the beach there always reminds him of his time in Hawaii. Waibun studied architecture in college, and he loves to take pictures and draw. He works at DES Architects, where he gets to turn drawings into real-life spaces.

ABOUT RAINBOW ROOSTER

RAINBOW ROOSTER
Travel Guide

If you've spent any time on O'ahu, you've probably met the island's unofficial mascot—wild chickens! We thought it would be fun to have a character as your guide. Who better to accompany you than the friendly, curious, free-spirited, and playful chicken who is always up for an adventure?

The chicken population has exploded over the years, especially after an enormous hurricane hit the islands in 1992. At that time, the strong winds freed some chickens from their coops. These chickens had babies with the native chickens brought by the Polynesians that are protected under state law. With no natural predators and no humans allowed to catch them, there's no one to stop them from multiplying!

And since a coloring book character needs color, with a little alliteration the chicken became......*Rainbow Rooster!*

Why we wrote this book

I love traveling to different places and have found incredible guidebooks, coloring books, and even comic books that teach me about the places I'm visiting. We looked for an interesting activity or guidebook for my Dad's hometown of Honolulu. We couldn't find one we loved, so we decided to create one together! We wanted to create a book that would be engaging, entertaining, and even educational!

How we wrote this book

I started by taking beautiful pictures of my favorite spots around the island, like the one to the left. As my Uncle Waibun and cousin Emily turned the photos into beautiful illustrations, my dad and I wrote descriptions of the sites and thought of recommendations we would give to our friends. We wanted to share these insider recommendations with you here. Enjoy your travels!

www.ingramcontent.com/pod-product-compliance
Lightning Source LLC
Chambersburg PA
CBHW041544120626
46551CB00019B/2837

9 7 9 8 9 9 3 4 6 5 4 8 7